PLAYFUL PHYSICS

DIY FUN PHYSICS EXPERIMENTS

ARJUN SARKAR

BlueRoseONE.com
Stories Matter
NewDelhi • London

BLUEROSE PUBLISHERS
India | U.K.

BlueRose ONE
Stories Matter
NewDelhi • London

For permissions requests or inquiries regarding this publication,
please contact:

BLUEROSE PUBLISHERS
www.BlueRoseONE.com
info@bluerosepublishers.com
+91 8882 898 898
+4407342408967

ISBN: 978-93-7139-379-9

Cover Design: Aman Sharma
Typesetting: Pooja Sharma

First Edition: July 2025

Preface

Through this book, I aim to educate and explain a variety of Physics (and some Chemistry) topics to middle-schoolers. This book follows a highly experiment-based approach to education, each topic is explained through its own experiment, with a proper learning lesson for each experiment. The main reason I chose to write this book is because, in my opinion and my prior experience, the sciences (specifically Physics and Chemistry), are taught through sheer memorization and mathematical formulas, this book aims to use real-world experiments to explain these concepts to middle-schoolers, solidifying their understanding of these topics. Moreover, this experiment-based approach will help plant the seeds of curiosity within the minds of students as they see the miracles and oddities of our world through a scientific Lense, ensuring a future full of scientific discovery and passion.

Acknowledgements

I would like to acknowledge and thank my parents, my Physics teacher Dhanraj sir, and my college advisors Geeti and Kanika ma'am for guiding me through the process of brainstorming ideas, effectively communicating them through this book, and helping me put it up on the market. The help I received from these individuals has been instrumental in ensuring the successful and smooth publication of my book.

Author Biography

Arjun Sarkar *is a senior student at Pathways World School, Gurgaon, pursuing the International Baccalaureate (IB) Diploma Programme with Higher Levels in Physics, Mathematics, and Global Politics. He is the author of Playful Physics, a student-led initiative designed to make core physics concepts accessible through interactive experiments and creative storytelling. Arjun's academic curiosity is matched by a hands-on approach to learning—his research paper "The Holes in Our Universe" was published in the IJARESM journal (ISSN: 2455-6211), and he continues to explore intersections of science and education.*

A former national-level participant in the F1 in Schools competition and an experienced karting athlete, Arjun is equally committed to technical design, having trained in Autodesk Fusion 360 and produced STEM outreach content on Medium and YouTube. His ongoing work emphasizes science communication for younger learners and interdisciplinary engagement. He also actively mentors children through physics demonstrations, bridging the gap between theory and fun.

For collaborations, school workshops, or support related to Playful Physics, Arjun can be contacted at ***arjunsarkarmusic@gmail.com****.*

Contents

Experiment 1: Balloon-Powered Car

Key concepts Kinetic energy, Potential energy Conservation of energy, Newton's laws of motion

Things Required:

- Plastic bottle
- Four plastic bottle caps
- Wooden skewer
- Two straws
- Balloon
- Tape
- Scissors or sharp knife (Have an adult use or supervise your use of this tool.) An adult helper

Steps:

1. Cut one of the straws in half.
2. Tape both pieces of the straw to one side of the water bottle.
3. Cut the wooden skewer in half and push each piece through one of the straws. These will form your axles. (Have adult help.)
4. Have an adult help use the scissors to poke a "+"-shaped hole directly in the center of each plastic bottle cap.
5. Press each bottle cap onto the ends of the wooden skewers. These will form your wheels.

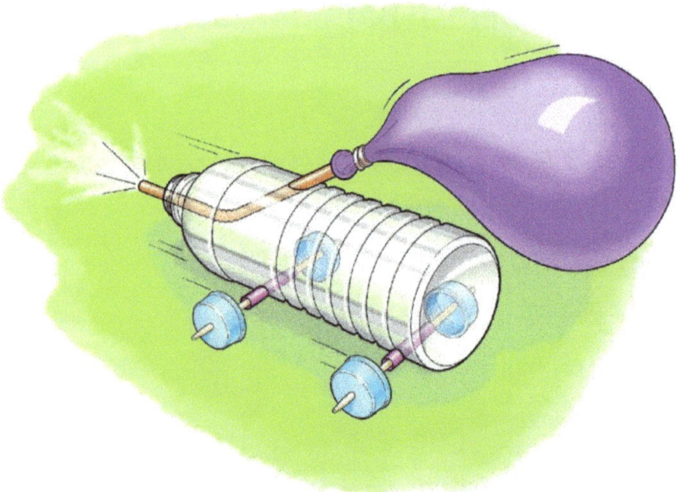

6. Put your car down on a flat surface and give it a good push. Make sure the car rolls easily and coasts for a bit before stopping. If your car gets stuck or does not roll smoothly make sure: your axles are parallel to each other; the hole in each bottle cap is centered; and the straws are securely taped to the

water bottle and do not wobble. You can add some glue if tape is not sufficient.

7. Tape the neck of the balloon around one end of the other straw. Wrap the tape very tightly so the connection is airtight.
8. Cut a small hole in the top of the water bottle, just big enough to push the straw through.
9. Push the free end of the straw through the hole and out the mouth of the bottle.
10. Use tape to secure the straw to the bottle.
11. Blow through the straw to inflate the balloon, then put your finger over the tip of the straw to trap the air.

Learning Lessons:

When you inflate a balloon and let it go, it zips randomly around the room. When you tape the balloon to a straw and attach it to the body of your car, however, you can control the direction of the escaping air. When the end of the straw is aimed backward, the air pushes your car forward, as described by Newton's third law of motion. Your design will be most efficient if the straw is pointed straight back and not downward or to the side. The more you inflate the balloon the more potential energy it stores, which in turn is converted to more kinetic energy, according to the law of conservation of energy—so the car will go faster.

When you inflate a balloon, it stores potential energy in the form of stretched rubber and the compressed air inside. When you release the balloon, this energy is converted to kinetic energy—the energy of motion—as the balloon zooms around the room.

Some of the energy is also converted to heat due to friction. According to the law of conservation of energy, the total amount of energy is conserved. Energy never "disappears"—it just changes to another form.

Another way to think about the balloon's movement is to use Newton's third law of motion: For every action there is an equal and opposite reaction. When you inflate a balloon and then release the nozzle, the rubber contracts and pushes the air out the nozzle. This means that there must be an equal and opposite reaction—the air pushes back on the rubber, propelling the balloon forward. This principle is used in real rockets and jets that shoot a high-speed stream of gases out the back of their engines, propelling the vehicle forward. In this project you will use this principle to build a toy car that is propelled forward by the stream of air escaping a balloon as it deflates.

What do you think will happen when you put the car down and release your finger?

7 Put the car down on a flat surface and release your finger. What happens?

7 See what adjustments you can make to make the car go farther.

7 What happens if you inflate the balloon more?

7 What happens if you adjust the direction the straw is aimed? Does it work best if the straw is aimed straight back?

Experiment 2: The Solar Oven

Key Concepts – Heat Energy, Absorption, Reflection , Conversion

Things Required:

- Cardboard pizza box
- Box knife or scissors
- Aluminum foil
- Clear tape
- Plastic wrap
- Black construction paper
- Newspapers
- Ruler or wooden spoon
- Thermometer
- An adult to help with cutting

Steps:

1. Use a box knife or sharp scissors to cut a flap in the lid of the pizza box. Cut along three sides, leaving about an inch between the sides of the flap and the edges of the lid. Fold this flap out so that it stands up when the box lid is closed.
2. Cover the inner side of the flap with aluminum foil so that it will reflect rays from the Sun. To do this, tightly wrap foil around the flap, then tape it to the back, or outer side of the flap.
3. Use clear plastic wrap to create an airtight window for sunlight to enter the box. Do this by opening the box and taping a double layer of plastic wrap over the opening you made when you cut the flap in the lid. Leave about an inch of plastic overlap around

the sides and tape each side down securely, sealing out air. If you use a plastic bag, cut out a square big enough to cover the opening and tape one layer over the opening.

4. Line the bottom of the box with black construction paper. Black absorbs all known wavelengths of light and converts them to thermal energy (heat). The black surface is where your food will be set to cook. How much you need will depend on the size of the pizza box you're using to make your solar oven.
5. To insulate your oven so it holds in more heat, roll up sheets of newspaper and place them on the bottom of the box. Tape them down so that they form a border around the cooking area. It may be helpful to also tape the rolls closed first. The newspaper rolls should make it so that the lid can still close, but there is a seal inside of the box, so air cannot escape.
6. The best hours to set up your solar oven are when the Sun is high overhead—from 11 am to 3 pm. Take it outside to a sunny spot and adjust the flap until the most sunlight possible is reflecting off the aluminum foil and onto the plastic-covered window. Use a ruler to prop the flap at the right angle. You may want to angle the entire box by using a rolled-up towel.
7. You can make toast by buttering a slice of bread then letting the Sun do the rest. Cooking a hot dog or making nachos with chips and cheese are also fun treats to make in your solar oven! It would also work great to heat up leftovers. So the paper at the bottom doesn't get dirty, put what you would like to cook on a clear plastic or glass plate. A pie plate would work well. Place the thermometer inside your oven before you close it, so you can check the temperature.
8. To take food out of the oven, open up the lid of the pizza box, and using oven mitts or potholders, lift the glass dish out of the oven.

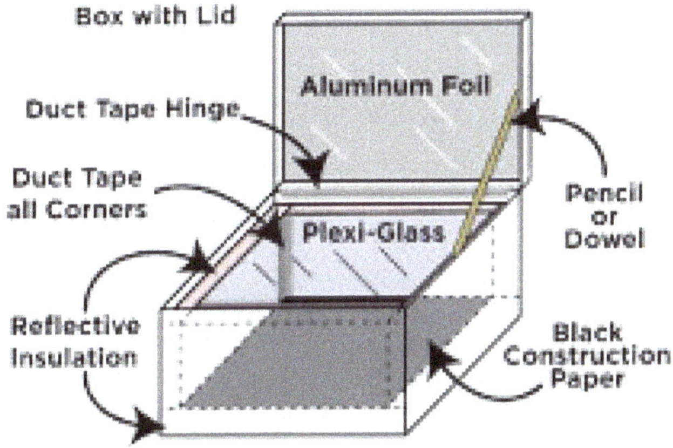
Box with Lid
Aluminum Foil
Duct Tape Hinge
Duct Tape all Corners
Plexi-Glass
Pencil or Dowel
Reflective Insulation
Black Construction Paper

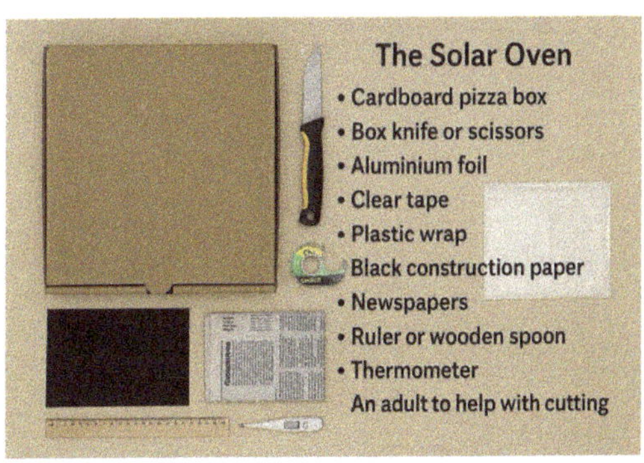
The Solar Oven
• Cardboard pizza box
• Box knife or scissors
• Aluminium foil
• Clear tape
• Plastic wrap
Black construction paper
• Newspapers
• Ruler or wooden spoon
• Thermometer
An adult to help with cutting

Learning Lessons:

The heat from the Sun is trapped inside of your pizza box solar oven, and it starts getting very hot. Ovens like this one are called collector boxes because they collect the sunlight inside. As it sits out in the Sun, your oven eventually heats up enough to melt cheese, or cook food! How does it happen? Rays of light are coming to the Earth at an angle. The foil reflects the ray and bounces it directly into the opening of the box. Once it has gone through the plastic wrap, it heats up the air that is trapped inside. The black paper absorbs the heat at the bottom of the oven, and the newspaper makes sure that the heat stays where it is, instead of escaping out the sides of the oven.

In most cases, sunlight isn't hot enough to heat water or food. Here, solar cookers convert light energy into concentrated heat energy, and this energy is used for cooking food. The conversion of sunlight to heat energy occurs when the photons of light waves (A form of electromagnetic radiation) interact with molecules of the substance. The electromagnetic radiation emitted by the Sun have energy in them. When they strike, the energy causes the molecules of the matter to vibrate. The molecules get excited and move to higher energy states. This activity produces heat.

Your pizza box solar oven can reach about 366.483 Kelvin on a sunny day and will take longer to heat things than a conventional oven. Although this method will take longer, it is very easy to use, and it is safe to leave alone while the energy from the Sun cooks your food.

Experiment 3: Snowball Slingshot

Things Required:

- Plastic bottle with tapered neck (we used a squash bottle)
- Marker pen
- Tape
- Balloon
- Scissors
- Some "snowballs" to send flying: cotton wool balls, or scrunched tin foil works perfectly
- Paper
- Colouring pencils/felt tips Any other decorations to make your launcher as jazzy as possible

Steps:

1. Draw a circle around the neck of your bottle in marker pen.
2. Cut along the line you have drawn. To get started you have to stab a hole in the bottle first using the pointy end of your scissors. An adult should definitely do this part.
3. We're only using the top of the bottle here, so you can use the bottom part to play ping pong pick up! If you've made any sharp or jagged edges with your scissors, cover them up with sticky tape so that your slingshot is safe to hold and use.
4. Take off the cap and stretch the balloon over the mouth of the bottle. If your balloon bunches up when you do this, gently pull it, so that it's even all the way round. Now is the time to test your launcher.

5. We recommend launching rolled up bits of tin foil or cotton wool balls so your home remains unscathed. And it should go without saying - don't fire them at each other!
6. Put your snowball into the bottle, hold onto the neck with one hand and pull the balloon back with the other. Then take aim and release the balloon to shoot snow through the sky.
7. Challenge your friends and family to see who can shoot the furthest and who has the best aim – we created targets on the floor, you can use bowls or boxes and place them wherever you like:

   An easy target scores 10 points

   Medium target, 20 points Difficult, 40 points
8. The competitor with the most points after five launches is the winner. Remember to play n-ice!

Learning Lessons:

Pulling the balloon back stretches it out of shape. When you let go, the balloon snaps back into its original shape, flicking into the snowball. This flicking force is what launches the snowball and sends it flying. But to win a game of Snowball Slingshot you need to know the best way to hold the tube. The secret is the direction, or angle, that you're pointing it.

This is because from the moment the snowball leaves the slingshot, the force of gravity controls the journey it takes. An object is called a projectile if, once it has been launched, the only force acting on it is gravity. So why does the angle that you fire your snowball make such a difference?

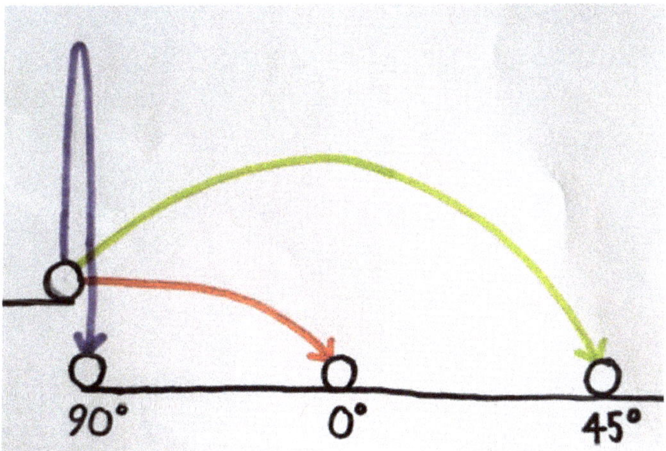

If you point straight upwards and launch, the snowball starts off quickly but the downwards pull of gravity causes the ball to travel slower and slower until it stops going upwards and starts to fall. The snowball speeds up as it falls back down and lands exactly where it started. Launching straight up like this keeps the snowball in the air for the longest time possible, but it hasn't gone forwards at all, which won't get you any points.

At the other extreme; when you point straight ahead and launch, we are pointing in the right direction. But because we aren't firing upwards at all, the snowball doesn't stay in the air very long so it doesn't go very far.

When you tilt the tube diagonally upwards and then launch, it's a compromise between the two and the snowball takes a curved path up and back down to the floor. To get the maximum distance and the most points you should launch diagonally upwards at 45 degrees (or 0.25π radians if you prefer radians to degrees). This angle is exactly between straight up and straight forwards and is the perfect balance between the two.

Knowing the physics behind snowball (or any projectile) launching should give you the secret to winning a game of snowball slingshot. It's up to you whether you decide to tell your family and friends!

Experiment 4: A Vortex Bottle

Things Required:

- Two empty clear plastic soda bottles
- A washer & Some duct tape

Steps:

1. Fill one of the bottles about 2/3 full with water, place the washer on the mouth of this bottle.
2. You can make the vortex more visible by adding a little food color to the water or some glitter or little foam beads.
3. Next invert the second bottle onto the washer and tape them together firmly.
4. Turn the two bottles over so the full one is on top. Swirl the bottle vigorously to start the water spinning.
5. Set the bottles down and watch the vortex form.
6. See how big you can make the vortex by spinning the water faster.
7. Experiment with washers that have different size holes.
8. See what happens when you tilt the bottle after a vortex has formed

Learning Lessons:

The tornado you see is actually a vortex. In a vortex, the fluid on the outside has to move faster than the fluid on the inside to keep up. This is why strong winds can be felt far away from the tornado and the eye of a hurricane is calm. The swirling water is creating a water vortex. The vortex is a funnel shape with a hollow center, just like a tornado. As such, the air from the bottle below can now pass unrestricted through the center of the vortex and into the bottle above.

Another experiment that you can do with vortices is quite simple and yet demonstrates an important principle of meteorology.

What you need: A large mug or a small pot, A spoon, Some ice

Pour some very hot water into the cup or pot and stir it slowly in one direction so the water is rotating slowly (you may want to put some food color in so you can see the water better). Next place a small ice cube at the center of the rotating water. With a little luck you should see the ice cube start to spin faster and faster until it is turning much faster then the water around it. What's going on?

This occurs because the melting ice causes water to sink underneath it. This in turn draws in some of the warm water from the top edges. This water coming in from the edges is what spins the ice cube faster. This is the same principle that causes some tornadoes and whirlpools in rivers to spin up. You may have to experiment with the position of the ice cube to make this work well. But then, experimentation is half the fun!

Experiment 5: Smoke Rings

Things Required:

- Cardboard Box (shoe box or tissue box works well)
- Plastic wrap
- Tape
- Baby powder or matches

Steps:

1. Take a cardboard box (a shoe box or tissue box works well) that is open on one side only.
2. Cover the open side with some plastic wrap (like Saran wrap) and tape it on well.
3. On the opposite side of the box cut a round hole 3 or 4 inches across.
4. You now have your smoke-ring maker so it's time to load it with smoke. This part can be dangerous so please ask an adult to help. There are many ways to get "smoke" into your smoke-ring maker; you can put a piece of "dry ice" into the machine (don't touch the dry ice with your skin, it is very, very cold), you can use some baby powder, if it is fine enough, or you can use smoke (but be careful that you don't light your box on fire!). You don't need much smoke to make many rings.
5. Once your machine is loaded you are ready to start experimenting. To make a smoke ring just tap the plastic covered side. What would happen if the hole were square?
6. What happens when your smoke rings hit something like a stick? Try making two smoking machines and then try sending the rings at each other. What happens when two smoke rings collide? (It's

hard to make them collide so you may have to work at it for a while.)

7. Try different methods for making the rings easier to see (like shining a flashlight on them). Can you think of more experiments for your smoke-ring machine?

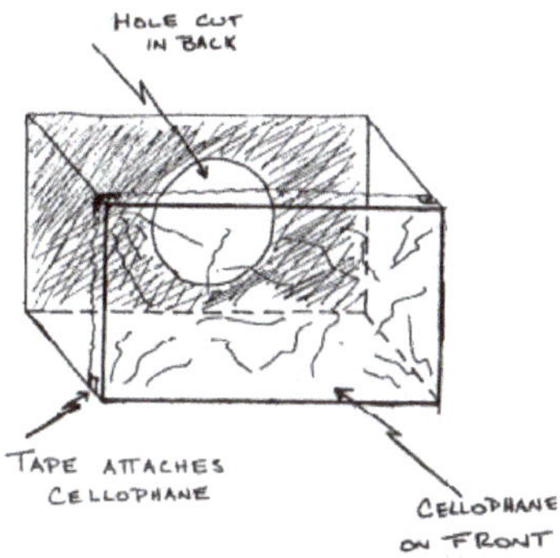

Learning Lessons:

A smoke ring is commonly formed when a puff of smoke is suddenly injected into clear air, especially through a narrow opening. The outer parts of the puff are slowed by the still air (or by edges of the opening) relative to the central part, imparting it the characteristic poloidal flow pattern. Since the air inside the vortex is moving faster than the outside air, the resulting inward pressure is the force that holds the smoke ring together. Eventually, air friction steals away all the energy stored in the vortex and the smoke ring drifts to a stop.

Experiment 6: Humpty Dumpty had a Great Fall

Things Required:

- 2-litre drinking glass,
- Water,
- Cake Pan,
- Cardboard,
- Toilet paper roll
- Ice (optional)
- Egg

This experiment will be messy, so find a space where your family is okay with you doing the experiment because you may crack a few eggs during the first couple of tries.

Steps:

1. Fill the glass with water
2. Place a pie pan right-side up on top of the glass
3. Place the toilet paper roll vertically in the middle of the pie pan
4. Balance the egg on top of the toilet paper roll so the egg is lying on it's side
5. Once everything is balanced on top of each other, with one swift and quick motion, hit the side of the pie pan with your hand. This is a horizontal swing, not a vertical swing. This needs to be enough force to push it off the glass.
6. Watch in amazement as your egg falls into the glass unbroken.

Learning Lessons:

How it Works:

It's all about Inertia & Newton's Laws of Motion

What are Newton's Laws of Motion?

An object at rest remains at rest, and an object in motion remains in motion at constant speed and in a straight line unless acted on by an unbalanced force. It's also called the Law of Inertia

Inertia says an object, the egg in this case, will stay at rest, unless an outside force acts upon it, your hand in this case. When you move the pie pan with your hand, gravity takes over and pulls the egg straight down into the glass of water.

Experiment 7: Catch The Coin

Things Required:

- Playing card
- Coin

Steps:

1. Place the cup upright on a table.
2. Now place the playing card over the opening of the cup.
3. Put the coin on top of the card.
4. Grab the edge of the playing card, and pull it quickly.
5. The coin should fall into the cup as opposed to flying across the room.
6. Try placing objects of different sizes, shapes, and weights on the playing card. Try things other than a playing card that have different textured surfaces. Try removing the playing card at different speeds.

Learning Lessons:

The coin wants to remain at rest because it has inertia. If you try to slowly pull the card away, you won't overcome the static frictional force and the coin will remain on the card. However, If you pull the card away quickly, the coin will stay in one place for a split second before gravity takes over and the coin falls into the cup.

Experiment 8: Floating Fish

Things Required

- A clean glass plate or dish
- Water
- Markers.

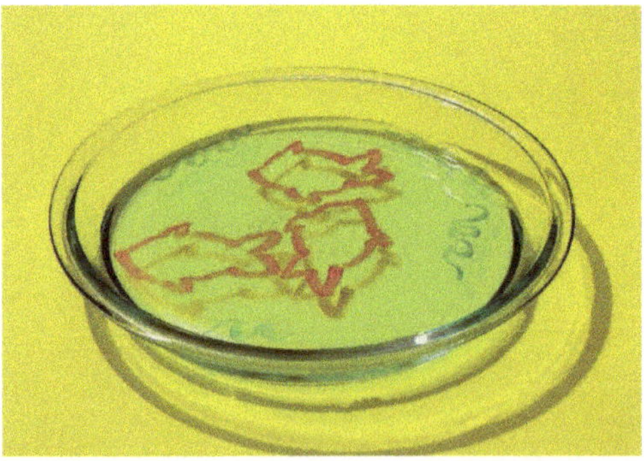

Steps:

1. Draw the outline of a fish on the bottom of a glass plate or tray in dry-erase marker.
2. Retrace your drawing to make sure all the lines are connected. Let dry for a minute or two.
3. Fill the measuring cup with tap water. Place the pour spout just inside the corner of the dish and add water very slowly until it just covers the bottom.
4. Be careful not to pour water directly onto your drawing or make splashes near it. The water will move toward your drawing, eventually surrounding it.
5. Observe what happens. If the water splashes or it doesn't work on your first try, empty the dish, erase the drawing with a paper towel, dry off the dish, and try again.
6. Tilt the dish slightly from side to side. What happens? Jot it down.

Learning Lessons:

The ink in dry erase markers is engineered to be slippery. It's made with a chemical that causes it to release from surfaces easily. (Permanent markers are made with a chemical that makes the ink stick to surfaces, so be sure not to use these in your experiment!)

The easy-release ink lets go from a surface, but why does it float? There are two reasons. First, dry erase ink isn't soluble, which means it won't dissolve in water. Second, dry erase ink is less dense than the water, so it becomes buoyant, meaning it can float. When you tilt the dish, the fish moves around on the water's surface.

Experiment 9: Duck call

Things Required:

- 1 drinking straw
- 1 pair of scissors

Steps:

1. Flatten one end of the straw. Then cut this end to make it pointy.
2. Put the flattened end in your mouth and blow. The shorter the straw and the flatter the end, the easier it is to make it sound.

Learning Lessons:

In air, sound consists of waves of denser air, moving from the source of the sound. Here, the straw works like any wind instrument. Inside is a column of air that can be made into waves. The length of this column of air can be changed and thus different musical notes can be obtained.

The air inside the straw is made into waves by the homemade mouthpiece. When you blow, the two tips hit each other very frequently. Just as water waves start if you hit a water surface, sound waves start here when the mouthpiece hits the air. The sound waves spread out through the open end of the straw and reach your ears.

The air column in the straw, and anything else that can vibrate, can only do so at one or a couple of speeds and can thus only be heard as one or a couple of notes. Exactly how fast something can vibrate depends on a number of factors, but the factor that can change here is the length of the air column. A short straw gives a fast vibration and short sound waves, which we humans perceive as a high note.

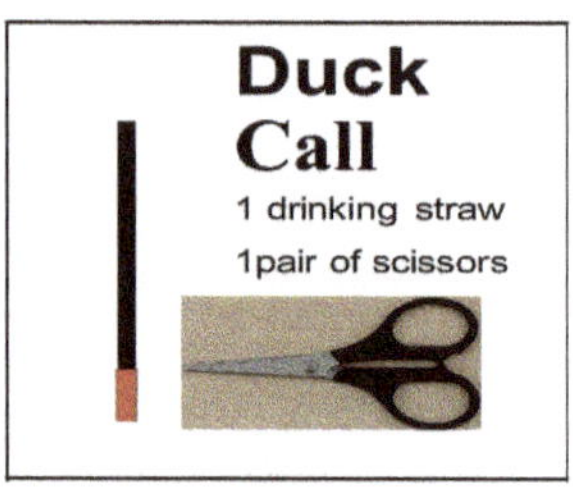

Experiment 10: Sticky Ice Science

Things Required:

- A piece of string
- three bowls.
- Ice
- Water
- Salt

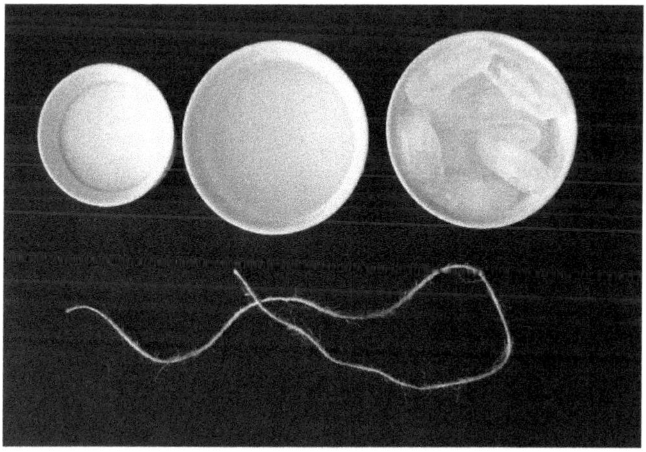

Steps:

1. Fill one bowl with a little water, one with ice and one with ice and salt
2. Cut a piece of string longer than the width of the cup.
3. Put it over the ice and try to lift ice.
4. Remove the string
5. Sprinkle salt over the ice cube
6. Lay the string over the ice cube.

7. Wait 60 seconds.
8. Carefully lift the string with the utmost concentration and watch as the ice comes along.

Learning Lessons:

The salt sprinkled on the ice causes it to start melting, just as salt added to icy roads does in winter. Water freezes at 32 degrees F (0 degrees Celsius) but when salt touches the ice, it lowers the freezing point to much lower than that. In order for the ice to melt, however, it has to absorb heat. The heat that it absorbs comes from what's around it, which in this case was the water near the ice cube.

Some of this water becomes so cold that it refreezes and the string becomes trapped. The string is now stuck and you can lift the cube out of the water. Try using different sized salt {rock salt, epsom, and table salt} to see if it has an effect on the time it takes the water to refreeze around the string. Try using a different type of salt {sodium bicarbonate aka baking soda} to see if it is as effective as table salt {sodium chloride}

Set up a control bowl of just ice and water as well as the salty ice water, use a thermometer or simply your finger to see if the addition of salt lowers the overall water temperature. You can use salt and ice to make homemade ice cream (Refer to Experiment 14).

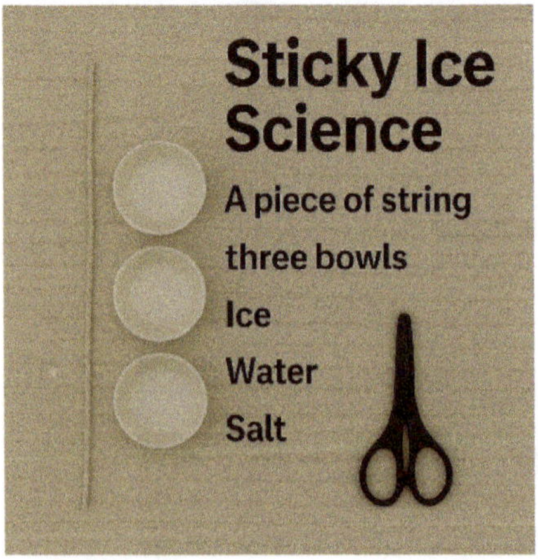

Experiment 11: Ice Cream Makers

Things Required:

- Measuring spoons
- Measuring cup
- Sugar
- Vanilla extract
- Salt. Different types of salts, such as table salt or rock salt, will all work, but may give slightly different results.
- Ice cubes (8 C)
- Small, sealable bags, such as pint-sized or sandwich-sized Ziplocs (2)
- Gallon-size sealable bags (2)
- Oven mitts or a small towel
- Timer or clock
- 1/2 a cup of half and half, cream, or milk

Steps:

1. In each small sealable bag, place one tablespoon of sugar, ½ cup of half-and-half (or milk or heavy whipping cream), and ¼ teaspoon of vanilla extract. Seal both bags well.

2. Add four cups of ice cubes to one of the large, gallon-sized bags. Then add ½ cup of salt to the bag. What will the salt do??

3. Put one of the small bags you prepared into the large bag with the ice cubes. Be sure both bags are sealed shut

4. Put on oven mitts or wrap the bag in a small towel and then shake the bag for five minutes. Feel the smaller bag every couple of minutes while you shake it, and take a peek at it.

5. Now add four cups of ice cubes to the other large, gallon-sized bag, but this time do not add any salt to it. What do you think will happen without using salt?

6. Put the other small bag you prepared into this large bag. Be sure both bags are sealed.

7. Put on oven mitts or wrap the bag in a small towel and then shake the bag for five minutes, as you did before. Again, feel the

smaller bag every couple of minutes while you shake it, and take a peek at it.

8. Think about:

    a. What happens to the ingredients over time now? When five minutes are up, how do they look now compared to last time? What about the ice cubes — did they change in the same way?

    b. You can also compare how cold the different ice cube bags feel. Does one feel much colder than the other?

    c. If you successfully made some ice cream, you can enjoy it now as a tasty reward for your chemistry challenge! If one of your bags did not make ice cream, check out the Further Exploration section for tips

Learning Lessons:

You should have seen that the ice cubes in the large bag with salt melted much more, and felt much colder, than the ice cubes in the large bag without salt. Because it was cold enough (several degrees below freezing), the ice cube bag with salt should have been able to cool the ingredients enough to harden them and turn them into ice cream. In contrast the ice cube bag without salt was not cold enough to do this and the ingredients should have remained fluid.

Do not worry, the second bag is not wasted — you can go back and turn the still liquid ingredients into ice cream! Simply put the small bag in the large bag that had ice cubes and salt and shake them for another five minutes.

If you have ever made ice cream with an old-fashioned hand-crank machine, you probably packed a mixture of ice and rock salt around the container holding the cream. The salt allows the ice and salt mixture to get colder than pure water ice. This extra-cold mixture of salt and ice is able to freeze the ingredients in the ice cream machine (and in the bags you used in this activity) and turn them into ice cream. (This is the same process that goes on when icy roads have salt spread on them to melt the ice.) While pure water freezes at 0 degrees Celsius (32 degrees Fahrenheit), water mixed with salt will freeze below 0 degrees Celsius.

In creating your ice cream you also made an emulsion. Emulsions are the combination of two liquids that normally do not mix well like fats and water. In your ice cream the fat molecules in the cream are perfectly mixed with water, ice crystals, sugar, and small pockets of air to form a delicious cold treat.

To understand how salt makes ice melt and makes things colder, let's look at ice itself. Ice is simply frozen water. For water to freeze and turn into ice, the tiny water molecules need to slow down and arrange themselves neatly.

When it's warmer, these molecules move around a lot — like excited little children — making it harder for them to line up properly. As the temperature drops, the molecules slow down, allowing them to form ice crystals more easily.

Even after ice has formed, two important things are always happening on its surface: the ice is melting, and the melted water is also freezing back into ice. The balance between how fast these two processes happen determines what you'll see.

Now, consider two bags of ice cream: one has just ice, and the other has ice mixed with salt. Both bags are in the same temperature environment, so the molecules in both bags are moving at the same speed. The big difference is the salt. As the ice starts to melt, the water mixes with the salt, which gets in the way of the water molecules trying to freeze back into ice. This means that the ice melts faster in the bag with salt because the process of refreezing is slowed down.

As the ice melts, it absorbs heat, making the surroundings colder. So, the bag with ice and salt actually gets colder than the bag with just ice. In fact, because the salt makes it harder for the water to freeze, a mix of salt and ice can go below the usual freezing temperature of water (0 degrees Celsius).

This phenomenon is called freezing point depression, meaning that the presence of salt lowers the freezing point of water compared to pure water. This concept isn't just limited to salt and water; it can happen with other mixtures as well!

For Further Exploration

- If one of your bags did not make ice cream, try putting it back in the large bag that had ice cubes and salt and then shake them for five minutes. Did it turn into ice cream? Why do you think you got the results that you did?
- Instead of half-and-half, you could use milk or heavy whipping cream to make ice cream in this activity. How does making ice cream with half-and-half compare to making it using milk or heavy whipping cream?
- You can make ice cream in this activity using different types of salts, but you may get different results. How does ice cream made in a bag with table salt compare to ice cream made with rock salt or some other type of salt? Can you explain your results?

Experiment 12: Playing Ping Pong by Yourself

Things Required:

- A ping pong ball
- A hair dryer
- Toilet Roll

Turn on the hair dryer and aim straight up.

Steps:

1. Place the ball above the hair dryer and watch it float in the air.
2. Put a toilet roll on a stick and place it above the hair dryer (you need a very strong hair dryer).
3. Then take the empty toilet roll, place it above a floating ping pong ball and see how the ball is sucked up through the toilet roll!
4. If you have a weak hair dryer, it works better with an inflated balloon instead of a ping pong ball. However, put a coin inside the balloon so it doesn't become too light!
5. If you don't have a hair dryer, you can make a miniature version of the demonstration. Take a straw with a bend and direct the bend straight upwards. Blow at the other end and then place a spun cotton ball in the air stream!

Learning Lessons:

This experiment illustrates Bernouille's principle. The principle states that the faster air moves over an object, the less the air pushes on the object (the air pressure is lower). Bernouille's principle explains how the ping pong ball remains in the air stream above the hair dryer. When the ball is in the air stream, it's surrounded by air with low air pressure. But if the ball tries to leave the air stream, it instead encounters the stagnant air around it. Since this air is stationary, it has a higher air pressure, i.e. pushes harder on the ball, and pushes the ball back into the air stream where the air pressure is low. The reason why the ball is also kept at a certain height is that the upward pressure of the air flow at that height balances the gravitational force on the ball.

Test the hypothesis by doing the experiment

- How much can you tilt the hair dryer without the ball falling down?
- How fast can you move the hair dryer sideways without the ball falling down?
- How many balls can you get in the air at one time?
- What other objects can you get to float above the hair dryer?

Experiment 13: Lava Lamps

Things Required:

- A clean plastic bottle, try to use one with smooth sides
- water
- Vegetable Oil (or you could use Mineral or Baby Oil instead)
- Fizzing tablets such as 'Eno' or 'Alka Seltzer'
- Food Coloring

Steps:

1. Fill the bottle up about 1/4th (1 quarter) with water.
2. Pour the vegetable oil in the bottle until it is almost full. You may want to use a measuring cup with a spout or a funnel. You may have to wait a couple of minutes for the oil and water to separate.
3. Add a few drops of your favorite food coloring. Watch as the color sinks through the oil. Did your drops of color mix with the water immediately or float in between for a few minutes?
4. Break your fizzy tablet in half and drop part of it into the bottle. Get ready … here come the bubbly blobs!
5. You can even get a flashlight, turn off the lights and drop in another half tablet. This time shine the flashlight through the lava lamp while the blobs are bubbling!

Learning Lessons:

The oil floats on top of the water because it is less dense or lighter than water. The food coloring has the same density as the water so it sinks through the oil and mixes with the water. When you add the tablet it sinks to the bottom then starts to dissolve. As it dissolves it makes gas, carbon dioxide. Gas or air is lighter than water so it floats to the top. The air bubbles bring some colored water with them to the top. When the air comes out of the colored water blob, the water gets heavy again and sinks. It does this over and over again until the tablet is completely dissolved.

Experiment 14: DIY Barometer

Things Required:

- An empty tin can
- Balloons (you may need a few – I'll explain why below)
- One thick rubber band
- A coffee stirrer or thin straw
- A paper clip & glue
- A ruler with metric measurements

Steps:

1. Cut the balloon about halfway down (you'll be using the larger portion of the balloon for the experiment, you may have to use more than one to get the correct sizing).
2. Stretch the cut balloon over the top of the tin can.
3. Secure the balloon using the rubber band so it won't slip off.
4. Unbend or straighten the paper clip.
5. Slide the paper clip into the coffee stirrer. It should fit in snuggly but if it's loose, be sure to glue it in place.
6. Glue the coffee stirrer to the center of your balloon so the end with the paper clip is hanging over the edge of the can.
7. Stand your ruler next to your barometer so the paper clip is pointing to the metric side of the ruler.
8. Record the date and the metric unit on the FREE Daily Barometer Record Log we've included below!
9. Be sure to put your barometer & ruler is a location where it doesn't have to be moved while you're tracking air pressure.

Lessons Learnt:

A barometer works by showing us whether the air pressure (or atmospheric pressure) is rising or falling. Atmospheric pressure is an indicator of what type of weather is occurring in your area. When the barometer readings fall, it indicates low pressure which usually shows in the way of clouds, winds and precipitation (so basically, a bad weather day. When the barometric pressure rises, it means fair weather (or a nicer day!) With a homemade barometer, the air is captured inside the can or jar once you secure the balloon to the top. So, as the air pressure outside the can changes, you will see the balloon either rise above the top of the can or sink into the can. If the air pressure outside of the can is less dense than the air inside the can (meaning air pressure is low), the balloon will expand, and the paper clip mark will drop lower on your ruler — low pressure means a better chance for rain and clouds. Conversely, if the air pressure outside the can is more dense (high pressure), than you'll see the balloon sink down into the can which will cause the coffee stirrer & paper clip to rise higher on your ruler — indicating nicer weather. Think of it this way — if the air is more dense (high pressure outside of the can), that means the molecules are pushing down on the balloon which causes it to sink into the can.

Experiment 15: Vanishing Coin

Things Required:

- A glass with straight sides
- Small jar or dish with a dip in the bottom (a concave part) – a ramekin is ideal
- A coin
- Water
- Jug for pouring
- Lid for your glass (can be anything to cover the top)
- Tea towel/ drying cloth

Before setting up the trick, it's important to know that it only works if you're looking at it from the side (not the top) so set up a chair for the members of your family you want to amaze and astound. Now you're ready to get started.

Steps:

1. To measure how much water you need, fill your glass all the way up with water then pour carefully into your jug.
2. Dry off your glass inside and out. Now you're set up.
3. Get your family or friends into position and introduce your trick.
4. Place the small jar upside down and the coin on top.
5. Place the glass on top of that. There should be a gap of air between your coin and your glass but your family should be able to see the coin. Make a big deal about how you can make it disappear.
6. Hold the lid open - but make sure your family can't see through the top of the glass.
7. Pour the water into your glass all in one go and drop the lid. Your coin should have vanished from view!
8. Once your family have recovered from the shock, lift the lid.
9. Illustration of a drinking glass on top of a dish. Image text reads jar or dish, drinking glass, lid table with plain surface works best, make sure jar isn't too tall or they will be able to see the coin from underneath, the glass must have straight sides, open lid towards you.

Learning Lessons:

Making the coin disappear might seem like magic, but like many optical illusions it only works if you're looking at it from a specific angle.

When you look at a coin normally, you can see it because light bounces off it in all directions and some of that light travels in a straight line to your eye.

In the first part of the trick, with the coin underneath the empty glass, things are a little bit more complicated. Light bouncing from the coin now has to travel through the air, the bottom of the glass, the air again, the side of the glass and – finally – though the air to your eyes.

Each time the light goes from one material to another it changes direction but most of it still gets through and so your family can still see the coin

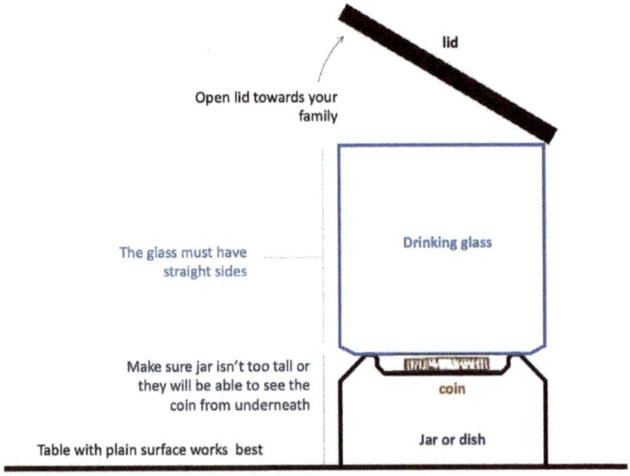

But only most of the light reaches your family, a small amount will be reflected off the side of the glass instead, bouncing back inside the glass and not reaching your eyes. Whether the light travels through a material or gets reflected depends on the angle the light is travelling at and the materials it is travelling between. That is why adding water to the glass is the final stage to our trick. The light from the coin at the bottom now has to travel through:

The air

The bottom of the glass The water

The side of the glass

The air again to your family

But the water changes the angle enough that instead of leaving the glass, all of the light is reflected. When 100% of the light reflects in this way, it's called total internal reflection. With the glass filled all the way to the top, none of the light from the coin at the bottom can escape through the sides. It’s trapped. It can never reach your eyes and so the coin seems to vanish.

Of course this only works if you’re looking through the side of the glass. We need a lid for the top so no one can see in. This is also why you need a straight-edged container; the size doesn’t matter, but it can’t have any curvy bits, or the light can "leak" out.

Knowing the physics behind what’s going on will help you set everything up, and soon you‘ll have all your family wanting to know the secret of the vanishing coin. Lifting the lid gives a clue – there's a very clear reflection of the coin, and if they look closely, the writing is back to front. Our five layers combine to make the perfect mirror.

Experiment 16: Build a Circuit

How to make a circuit? A circuit is a path that electricity flows along. It starts at a power source, like a battery, and flows through a wire to a light bulb or other object and back to the other side of the power source. You can build your own circuit and see how it works with this project!

Things Required:

- Small light bulb (or a flashlight bulb)
- 2 batteries (with the correct voltage for your light bulb)
- 2 alligator clip wires or aluminum foil*
- Paper clips
- Electrical tape (Scotch®tape also works)
- Bulb holder (optional)
- Battery holders (optional**)
- To use foil instead of wires, cut 2 strips each 6″ long and 3″ wide. Fold each one tightly along the long edge to make a thin strip.)
- To use paper clips instead of battery holders, tape one end of a paper clip to each end of your battery using thin strips of tape. Then connect your wires to the paper clips.

Steps:

Part 1 – Making a Circuit:

- Connect one end of each wire to the screws on the base of the light bulb holder. (If you're using foil, ask an adult to help you unscrew each screw enough to fit a foil strip under it.)
- Connect the free end of one wire to the negative ("-") end of one battery. Does anything happen?

- Attach the free end of the other wire to the positive ("+") end of the battery. Now what happens?

Part 2 – Adding Power

- Disconnect the battery from your circuit. Stand one battery so that the "+" end is pointing up, then set the other battery next to it so that the flat "-" end is pointing up. Tape around the middle of the batteries to hold them together.
- Set a paperclip across the batteries so that it connects the "+" end of one to the "-" end of the other. Tape the paperclip in place with a narrow piece of tape (do not tape over the metal battery ends).
- Turn the batteries over and tape one end of a paper clip onto each of the batteries. Now you can connect one wire to each paper clip. (The bottom of the battery pack should only have one paper clip – do not connect a wire to it.)
- Connect the free ends of the wires to the light bulb.

(Note: Instead of steps 1-3, you can use two batteries in battery holders and connect them together with one wire.)

What Happened:

In the first part, you learned how to make a circuit with a battery to light up a light bulb. Batteries supply electricity. When they're connected properly, they can "power" things, like a flashlight, an alarm clock, a radio… even a robot!

Why didn't the light bulb light up when you connected it to one end of the battery with a wire? Electricity from a battery has to flow out one end (the negative or "-" end) and back in through the positive ("+") end in order to work. What you built with the battery, wire, and bulb in step 3 is called an open circuit. In order for electricity to start flowing, you need a closed circuit. Electricity is caused by tiny particles with negative charges, called electrons.

When a circuit is complete, or closed, electrons can flow from one end of a battery all the way around, through the wires, to the other end of the battery. Along its way, it will carry electrons to electrical objects that are connected to it – like the light bulb – and make them work!

In the second part, you added another battery. That should have made the light bulb burn more brightly, because two batteries together can supply more electricity than just one! The paper clip across the bottom of the battery pack allowed electricity to flow between the batteries, making the flow of electrons stronger.

Build a Circuit

- Small light bulb (or a flashlight bulb)
- 2 batteries (with the correct voltage for your light bulb)
- 2 alligator clip wires or aluminum foil*
- Paperclips
- Electrical tape (Scotch® tape also works)
- Bulb holder (optional)
- Battery holders

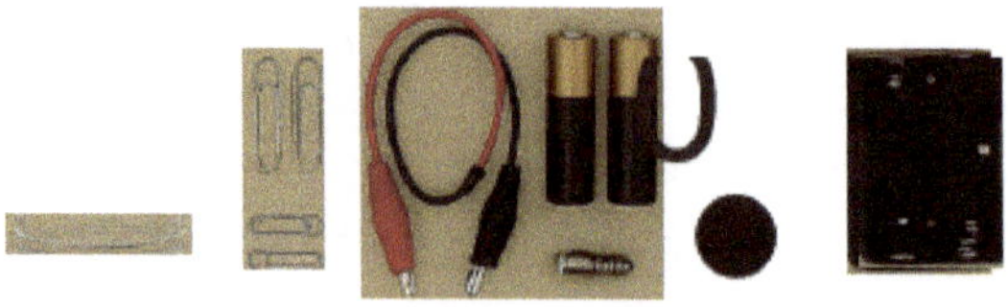

Experiment 17: Infinity Mirror

Things Required

- Mirror
- Plexiglass or acrylic sheet - You will need to cut the plexiglass sheet to size to fit your mirror. Adult supervision is recommended. It is relatively easy to cut a rectangular piece of plexiglass, but cutting a circle can be more difficult (see Procedure). Some vendors like McMaster-Carr sell pre cut plexiglass circles (click on "Optically clear and colored cast acrylic", then scroll down the page to the circular pieces).

Note: Several different brand names and materials are commonly called "plexiglass," such as acrylic and polycarbonate. Some of them have a different hardness or resistance to shattering. All that really matters for this project is optical clarity — make sure the plexiglass you buy is clear and not translucent or opaque.

- Mirrored window film
- Cardboard box or other container
- LEDs
- Power supply
- Tape or glue
- Cutting tool
- Safety glasses or protective goggles

1. The first decision you will need to make is how big and what shape you want your infinity mirror to be. This will determine the size and shape of the box or case you use, along with the regular mirror and piece of plexiglass.

2. Important: Be careful with box and mirror sizing. For example, a 6 inch diameter circular mirror will not necessarily fit inside a 6 inch diameter papier mâché box. Six inches could be the outer diameter of the box, and the inner diameter might be slightly smaller (for example, 5-7/8 inches). Remember that you can also use the lid of the box (which will be slightly larger), or build your own custom-sized box out of cardboard or cardstock.

3. You might want to use two boxes, one slightly larger than the other. This way, you can pack the wiring for your lights between the two boxes so you do not have extra wiring dangling from the outside of your infinity mirror.

4. Think ahead about how you will cut your plexiglass to the appropriate size and shape for your mirror, and what tools you will need

5. Important: Adult supervision is required when using sharp handheld tools or power tools. Always wear appropriate safety gear (e.g., eye protection) and follow all safety precautions for the equipment you are using.

6. In general, it is easier to cut rectangular pieces of plexiglass than circular or irregularly shaped pieces. You can do this by scoring straight lines in the plexiglass using a utility knife or special plastic-cutting knife, and then breaking the plexiglass along the scored line.

7. If you need to cut a circle, you can use a fine-toothed jigsaw blade or bandsaw. Some vendors sell precut circles of plexiglass (see the materials section for details).

8. In both cases, C-clamps are extremely helpful for safely holding the plexiglass down to the edge of a work table.

9. Determine what type of lights you want to use. Figure 5 shows several different light options.

10. You can figure out how many lights (or how long of a strand of them) you need by calculating the inside perimeter of your infinity mirror. For example, a 2x3 inch box has a perimeter of 10 inches.

11. Many strands of Christmas lights are sold in much longer lengths; for example 10, 25, or 50 feet [ft.] — more than you will probably need. You can still use a longer strand, but you will have to bundle up all the extra lights. Do not cut off any extra lights unless the instructions that come with the lights say it is OK to do so.

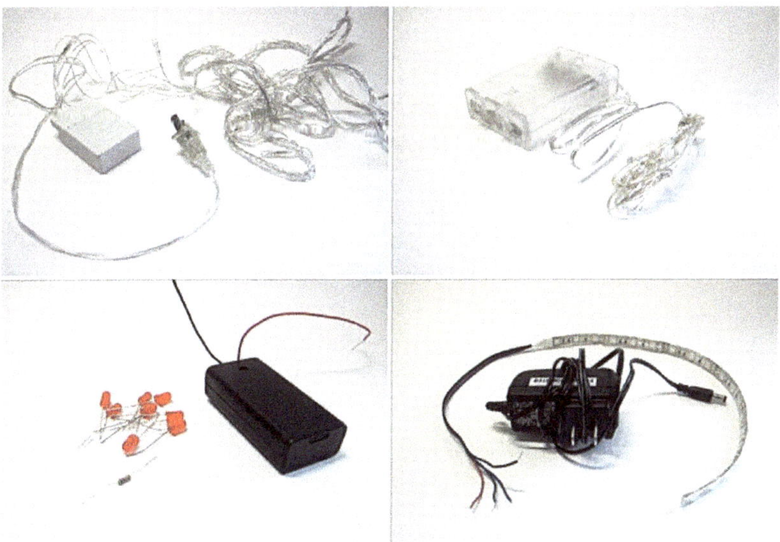

12. Certain LED strips can be cut to a shorter length, and some cannot. Be sure to read the product information before you purchase an LED strip, to make sure it will work for your project. For example, some LED strips can be cut to shorter lengths, but only in 3 inch segments. That will not work if the

inner diameter of your mirror is 8 inches, because 8 is not a multiple of 3.

13. If you are using individual LEDs, you will have to figure out how closely spaced you want them to be, and then purchase enough to fill your mirror. For example, if the inside perimeter of your mirror is 8 inches, and you want an LED placed every ½ inch, then you will need to buy 16 LEDs. You will also need additional materials (battery pack, connecting wire, a soldering iron, and a resistor) to connect them.
14. Figure out how you are going to attach all the different parts of your mirror. How will you attach the mirror to the inside of the cardboard box? What about attaching the plexiglass to the front? How will you hold the LEDs in place?
15. For example, you could use either double-sided tape or superglue to mount the mirror to the bottom of your box.
16. You could poke tiny holes in the sides of your box, stick the LEDs through, and let them be held in place by friction. Or, you could add some glue, using a hot glue gun to make sure they do not move around.
17. Think about the assembly process — remember that you want to be very careful not to get any glue on the surface of either mirror.
18. Plan ahead for how your infinity mirror will look. Are you OK with just a rough-looking mirror that you can use for a science project? Or do you want a nicer mirror that you can hang on the wall of your home? Will you want to paint the outside of your mirror a certain color, or make sure that there are no loose wires visible from the outside?
19. Once you have given some thought to everything mentioned in steps 1–5, make a complete list of materials and tools that you will need to build your mirror. You might have to make a trip to a hardware or arts and crafts store, or you can go back to the

Materials section for links to buy some of the parts online. Once you have all the parts, you are ready to move on to the next section and start building.

20. Building Your Infinity Mirror

21. Remember: This Procedure is a general set of guidelines to build an infinity mirror. Depending on the design of your mirror, you might not follow these steps exactly. If you think you have a better idea for how to build your mirror, try it your way instead.

22. As a first step, poke holes in the sides of the papier mâché box for your LEDs, as shown in Figure 7. You can do this with a sharp knife, a power drill, or even a pointy pen.

23. Note: If you purchased an LED strip, you may be able to mount it flat to the inside walls of the box, without making holes.

24. Next, mount the mirror inside the box using an adhesive. Figure 8 shows a mirror being mounted using double-sided foam tape, but you could also use glue.

25. Handle the mirror by the edges so you do not get any fingerprint smudges on it. Use a clean object, like a paper towel, to firmly press down on the surface of the mirror so it sticks to the tape.

26. Be very careful not to get any glue, or the sticky side of tape, on the surface of the mirror. The cleaner the mirror is, the better the optical illusion will look.

Insert the LEDs. How exactly you mount them will depend on the type of LEDs you are using.

If you just push the LEDs through the holes, they might not stay in place very well (see the top image) You can use a hot glue gun to attach the base of each LED to the box, holding it in place (center image).

27. You can use tape to bundle up all the excess wire on the outside of the box (bottom image). Remember to put this box inside a larger box to conceal all the extra wires.

    If you are using individual LEDs, remember that you will need to solder wire to connect them and the resistor, according to the circuit diagram

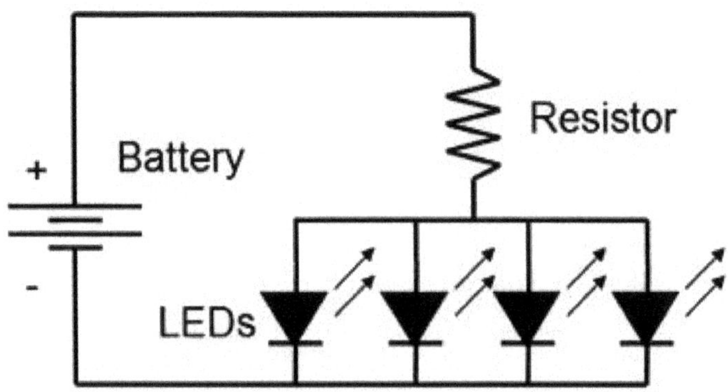

28. Use a hobby knife to cut a hole in the lid of the box
29. Cut your plexiglass to the appropriate size for your mirror. Adult supervision and protective eyewear are required for this step.
30. If you are cutting a rectangular piece of plexiglass, use a ruler and a utility knife (or a special plastic-cutting knife, which you can find at a hardware store) to score straight lines into the plexiglass. You will need to score the plexiglass deeply in order for it to break easily..

31. Hold the plexiglass at the edge of a table, preferably using C-clamps, and press down on it to snap off a piece. Repeat the process along each score line.

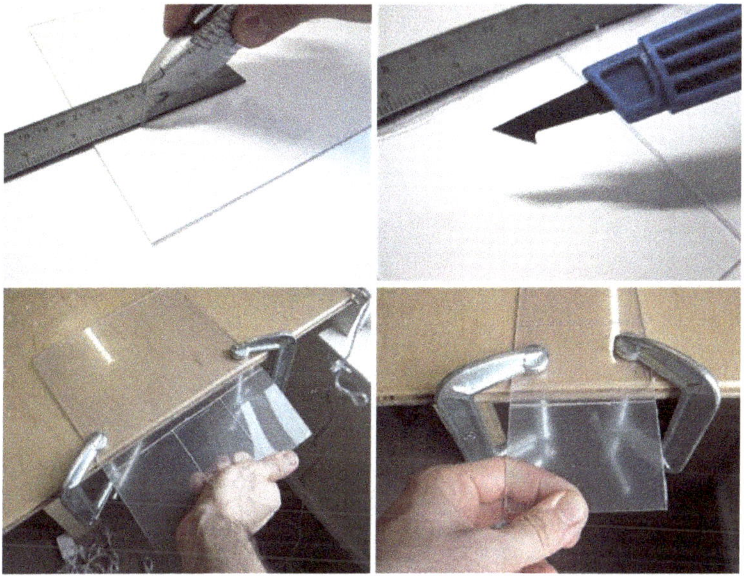

32. If you are having trouble breaking the plexiglass, try making a deeper score line. You can also store the plexiglass in the freezer for a few hours (this will make it more brittle) and then try again immediately after removing it from the freezer.

33. Apply the window film to the plexiglass (see the images in Figure 12).

34. Make sure you read the instructions for applying your window film. The instructions might vary depending on what kind you purchased.

35. Some window films recommend using water or a special spray as a lubricant to apply the film. Read the directions for your film and apply a lubricant to the plexiglass if necessary

36. Most window films come with an adhesive backing that will stick to windows. There is a protective covering on the adhesive

side. You will need to peel up one corner of this covering (top right image).

37. Carefully apply the window film to the plexiglass (center left image).

38. Do not use your fingers to smooth out the film — remember that you do not want to create smudges or fingerprint marks! Instead, use a paper towel, or a squeegee if you have one available. An index card or heavy business card will also work. Do your best to smooth out the film (center right image).

39. Use a utility knife to trim the excess film off around the edges of the plexiglass

40. If you need to cut a circular piece of plexiglass, have an adult help you use a jigsaw or a bandsaw with a fine-toothed blade (a rough-toothed wood-cutting blade will cause the plexiglass to shatter or crack).

41. Mount the plexiglass mirror to the inside of the box's lid, as shown in Figure 13.
42. You can do this using either glue (left image) or double-sided tape.
43. Mount the plexiglass with the window film facing in, meaning it will be facing the inside of the box when you put the lid on. This way you do not have to worry about the window film peeling or getting scratched from being the outside of the box.
44. Put the lid on the box

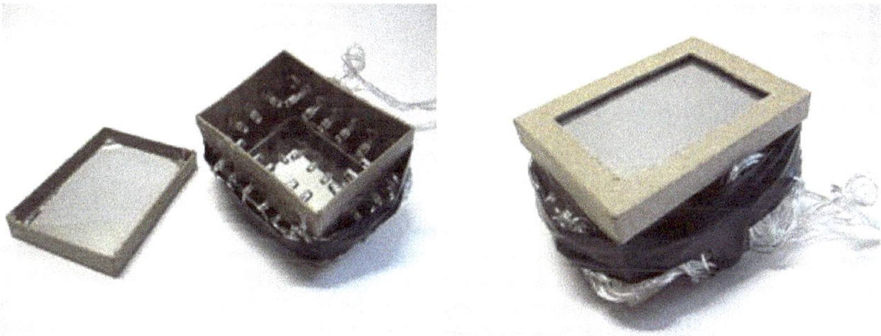

45. Plug the lights in and test out your infinity mirror. The "infinity" effect will work best in a dark room.

Troubleshooting

If your LEDs do not turn on, double check the power supply connection, especially if you soldered a circuit yourself. Make sure you have fresh batteries if your LEDs use batteries.

If your mirror appears smudged or dirty, try cleaning the plexiglass, mirror film, and regular mirror with window cleaner and a paper towel.

If there are "bubbles" distorting the image, this is probably because the mirror film is not completely flat against the plexiglass. Try re-applying mirror film to a new piece of plexiglass, and do your best to smooth it completely flat.

If your infinity tunnel appears to curve off to one side, this is because the plexiglass is not parallel to the regular mirror. Try adjusting the tilt of the lid slightly to straighten out the tunnel

Experiment 18: Make your Own Electromagnet

Things Needed

- 6 volt (V) lantern battery
- Enamel-coated magnet wire, 30 AWG (75 feet)
- Alligator clip leads (2)
- Iron bolts; about 2 1/2 inches long and 1/2 inch in diameter (4)
- You will also need to gather these items, not included in the kit:
- 220 grit sandpaper (about 1 square inch)
- Masking tape (1 roll)
- Box of steel paper clips (about 100 count)
- Scissors or wire cutters
- Optional: Shallow plastic container, slightly longer and wider than the iron bolts
- Recommended: A paper towel holder, or materials to make a simple spool holder for the magnet wire, like a pencil and a small cardboard box

Steps:

a. Make four different electromagnets—with 50, 100, 150, and 200 turns of wire, respectively—by tightly winding the magnet wire around the iron bolts (Figure 2). Here are some tips for making the magnets, but you can also refer to our How to Make an Electromagnet video for more details. If you have trouble, see the FAQ for more information.

b. Use a paper towel holder to hold the magnet wire spool while winding your magnets, or make an improvised one using a pencil and a cardboard box (Figure 3). This will help you keep your coils neat and prevent knots in the wire.

c. Leave a tail of wire—at least 6 cm long—at each end of the coil. You will use these wire tails to connect the coil to the battery.

d. Use small pieces of masking tape to attach each end of the coil to the bolt, to prevent it from unraveling.

e. Rotate the iron bolt to unwind the magnet wire from the spool. Do not pull the wire off the spool and wrap it around the bolt while still holding the bolt; this will cause the wire to get tangled. Use your fingers to keep the wire tight against the bolt, and wrap each successive turn tightly against the previous one. If these instructions are not clear, watch the video to see how to wind the magnet.

f. Your 50- and 100-turn coils should fit entirely on the smooth part of the bolt. The 150- and 200-turn coils will go onto the threaded part. This will make it more difficult to keep the turns neat and tightly packed against each other, because they will tend to go into the threads of the bolt, but this is okay.

g. Keep track of how many turns you make. This is easier if you use a piece of tape or a mark on the bolt so you can easily count one full rotation. It also helps to recruit a helper to make tally marks for you.

h. Use masking tape and a pen or fine-point marker to label each magnet with the total number of turns.

2. Use the 220-grit sandpaper to sand off 1 cm of the enamel insulation from both ends of each coil. To do this, cut a small piece of sandpaper, fold it in half, then pinch it around the wire and gently pull on the wire several times to remove the insulation. Watch this video for a more detailed explanation of how to strip the wires.

3. Testing Your Electromagnets
4. Make a data table, like the Table below , in your notebook.

Number of Turns	Number of Paper Clips Picked Up					
	1	2	3	4	5	Average
50						
100						
150						
200						

5. Place the paper clips in a small, shallow container. If you do not have a shallow container, put the paperclips in a pile on a flat surface.
6. Starting with the 50-turn coil, use the electromagnets to pick up paper clips from the shallow container.

7. Important: Your electromagnets will get hot if you leave them connected to the battery in between tests. Always disconnect one alligator clip when your electromagnets are not in use.

8. Connect one end of the red alligator clip to the "+" terminal of the battery, and the other end to one end of the wire coil. Make sure you connect to the part where you sanded off the insulation. Note: In electronics, it is standard convention to use red for positive and black for negative. Your electromagnet will still work regardless of which color alligator clip you use, but it is a good habit to practice!

9. Connect one end of the black alligator clip to the "-" terminal of the battery, and the other end to the free end of the wire coil. As soon as you do this, your electromagnet will turn on and begin to heat up, so it is important to work quickly.

10. Touch the head of the bolt to the pile of paper clips, and then pull the coil away from the tray . There should be some paper clips attached to the bolt. If it does not lift any paper clips at all, then your electromagnet is not working. See the FAQ for help.

11. Move the bolt away from the tray, and then disconnect one alligator clip (it does not matter which one, and you do not need to disconnect all four alligator clips). This should turn your electromagnet off and the paper clips should fall away from the bolt.

12. Count the number of paper clips that the magnet picked up, and record this value in your data table.

13. Return all of the paper clips to the container.

14. A small electromagnet presses against paperclips in a bowl
15. Repeat step 3 four more times, for a total of five trials.
16. Repeat steps 3–4 for the 100, 150, and 200-turn coils. Always remember to disconnect your electromagnets from the battery when not in use.
17. Analyze your data.
18. Calculate the average number of paper clips picked up for each number of turns in the coil.
19. Make a graph of the results. Plot the number of paper clips picked up (y-axis) versus the number of turns in the coil (x-axis). If you need help making a graph, try using the Create a Graph website.
20. Does the number of paper clips picked up increase or decrease as you increase the number of turns in the electromagnet?